DISCOVER
Your Career

Careers If You Like the Creative Arts

Stuart A. Kallen

ReferencePoint Press
San Diego, CA

ReferencePoint Press®

Printed in the United States

For more information, contact:
ReferencePoint Press, Inc.
PO Box 27779
San Diego, CA 92198
www.ReferencePointPress.com

LIBRARY OF CONGRESS CATALOGING-IN-PUBLICATION DATA

Names: Kallen, Stuart A., 1955– author
Title: Careers If You Like the Creative Arts / by Stuart A. Kallen.
Description: San Diego, CA : ReferencePoint Press, Inc, 2026. | Series: Discover Your Career| Includes bibliographical references and index. |
Identifiers: LCCN 2025038090 (print)
9781678212162 lib. bdg. | ISBN 9781678212179 ebook
Subjects: LCSH: Juvenile literature | Vocational guidance

For compete cataloging-in-publication data please go to www.loc.gov.

Contents

Introduction: Inspiration Occupations

People who work in creative occupations use their imaginations when solving problems. They start with what they know about a situation, add fresh new ideas, and look at old concepts from a different perspective. And sometimes creative people change the world. Computer scientist Tim Berners-Lee relied on his creative instincts when he invented the World Wide Web.

In 1989 Berners-Lee saw that computers were increasingly important in education and business. But computers often ran on different operating systems, which made them incompatible with one another. Berners-Lee said he wanted to connect all the computers together in one big web: "When I thought about the system I wanted to build, I wanted an instrument for collaboration, for remote creativity, for learning, and for connecting. I wanted to connect people to one another, anywhere in the world, and help them share their ideas."[1] This inspired vision prompted Berners-Lee to study existing technology, including the internet and various computer languages, that could be used to build websites and link them together. As Berners-Lee wrote in 1999, "Inventing the World Wide Web involved my growing realization that there was a power in arranging ideas in an unconstrained, weblike way. And that awareness came to me through . . . the swirling together of influences, ideas, and realizations from many sides."[2]

Thanks to the creative mind of Berners-Lee, there are now millions of jobs available to those who love swirling together influences, ideas, and realizations. People with a passion for the creative arts can construct careers based on their designing, drawing, or writing talents while using the web to develop new concepts and promote their work. Some pick up tools like cameras and movie equipment or musical instruments and recording gear to build careers based on their creative impulses. Those who like to work with their hands can bring up tutorials, podcasts, and other digital information to improve their pottery, jewelry, floral arrangements, and other craftwork.

Creative Jobs Everywhere

In 2025 the Bureau of Labor Statistics (BLS) said that around 2.6 million Americans make their living in a broad category called arts, entertainment, and recreation. The performance art category includes actors, singers, dancers, musical groups, and other entertainers. The classification also includes those who produce and promote events, manage entertainers, produce music, and provide artistic, creative, and technical skills to the film and television industries. The BLS says that another million or so people use their creativity every day in design occupations. These workers in the graphics, fashion, advertising, and interior design industries create products that are both practical in nature and visually pleasing. Imaginative people are also in high demand in the tech industry. There, industrial designers, animators, and video game producers meld their flair for science and technology with their artistic instincts.

Pursuing a creative career requires determination, persistence, hard work, and imagination. Thinking outside the box is not always easy, as marketing brand strategist Liz Marie can attest: "You have to be creative all the time. You are literally getting paid for this. Your livelihood depends on your creativity. . . . And that is a lot of pressure."[3] Liz Marie also points out that her job requires her to use her creativity in a business setting. That means sometimes putting aside her big artistic concepts to create products that satisfy clients and her employer.

On balance, Liz Marie says if you have a creative mind and artistic instincts, you would probably be painting, designing, writing, or playing music anyway. "So to get paid for it is really cool! And it doesn't always feel like work. Sometimes it feels fun; it feels like a creative puzzle. It can really fill you up."[4]

Finding Your Purpose

Many people dream of having a job that is fun and does not always feel like work. And multiple studies have shown that people who work in artistic careers have a greater overall sense of happiness compared to those who work in offices and factories. Psychologist Steve Taylor says this is because people need to feel as if they are doing something meaningful with their lives. "By pursuing meaning and purpose in your job, you'll feel that you're working toward a greater cause and mission," he writes. "When you feel that you are on a mission, work doesn't feel like drudgery. This mindset will energize you and provide inner joy and satisfaction from doing something important."[5]

Some creative jobs provide more sense of purpose than others. But the average person works around forty hours a week. If your mind is occupied every day by new challenges and new creative opportunities, that time can fly by and feel as if it is well spent.

Craft Artist

What Does a Craft Artist Do?

In 2025 the e-commerce website Etsy had more than 95 million active buyers and attracted over 400 million visitors every month. Etsy offers customers an astonishing array of unique handmade items created by craft artists, including jewelry, quilts, clothing, pottery, toys, furniture, photos, and paintings. Other e-commerce sites, like Amazon Handmade and Goimagine, offer similar creations made by artists who have built careers doing what they love.

Craft artists make handmade objects that are designed to be useful as well as artistically pleasing. They use raw materials that might include wood, metal, clay, paints, paper, fabric, and gems. Craft artists are weavers, clothing makers, toy makers, woodworkers, metalworkers, calligraphers, fiber artists, carvers, potters, jewelers, glassblowers, furniture makers, illustrators, and goldsmiths.

Visit any e-commerce craft website and you will be struck by the incredible diversity of products. Jewelers might specialize in making a particular type of ornament, such as necklaces, rings, earrings, bracelets, anklets, and arm bands. A craft artist might focus on a single accessory like a belt, while

At a Glance

Number of Jobs
54,000 in 2023

Pay
$38,480 for craft artists in 2024

Educational Requirements
None

Personal Qualities
Creativity, artistic abilities, business skills

Working Conditions
Irregular hours, including nights and weekends, sometimes working with hazardous materials

Future Job Outlook
Growth of 3 percent through 2033

others make hats, gloves, key chains, headbands, and even sunglasses. Artists who concentrate on home decor make pillows, wall and table decorations, candles, dried floral arrangements, etched glasses, hand-painted plates, lamps, tables, and chairs. The range of outdoor and garden items includes handmade planters, birdhouses, plant stands, and mailboxes.

In addition to selling their goods on e-commerce platforms, craft artists pursue other sales opportunities. Almost every midsize to large city hosts a craft fair, street fair, or art festival where craft artists set up sales booths and other displays. Craft artists also exhibit their goods in boutiques, restaurants, galleries, and consignment craft stores, with the owners of these businesses taking a percentage of each sale.

A Typical Workday

Prospective craft artists dream of spending their days in sunny art studios lovingly fashioning artistic works. In this vision they keep their own hours and tune out the world while they focus their creative energies on making beautiful art objects. While this dream is a reality for some, making art is only part of the job. And ignoring the outside world is not an option for those who want to maintain a successful business.

Craft artists need to juggle many tasks in a day. Some prefer to follow their creative impulses during the early mornings, when all is quiet and work can proceed undisturbed. Later in the day, hours might be spent on business activities, which can take up more time than making art. An embroidery artist named Alex explains, "My workday usually involves checking emails, packing orders, putting [embroidery] kits together and ordering supplies, and sometimes I even get to actually stitch something! I seem to spend more time these days on the computer. . . . I joke a lot that for someone with a creative business it doesn't always feel like I'm creating much."[6]

Art and Business

"When I first started [working as an illustrator] full-time, I pretty much drew all the time, shared to social media a few times a week and wrote the odd newsletter. Looking back now at the luxury of 10 hours a day of drawing, I realize . . . how blessed I was. . . . Very soon the marketing and customer service side of my business did take over. My day became one of two halves. During the day I would be working on my marketing plan, social media and customer service, usually around 4 hours a day, then I would start my drawing, usually early evening and work into the night."

—Bonny Snowdon, illustrator

Bonny Snowdon, "The Story of a Full-Time Artist," Bonny Snowdon Academy, May 3, 2024. https://bonnysnowdonacademy.com.

In addition to the tasks mentioned by Alex, craft artists also spend time texting and calling current or prospective clients, filling out invoices, paying bills, and dealing with taxes and other non-creative issues. Some craft artists boost their income by hosting workshops where local amateurs pay for instruction and perhaps a dose of inspiration. Hosting workshops can be a full-time job in itself; the artist needs to book a location, advertise to attract attendees, and prepare lessons and demonstrations.

Most craft artists need to spend time promoting themselves and their work. Painter and art business authority Eric Rhoades says creative artists should spend at least 20 percent of their time on marketing tasks. These tasks include building and maintaining a personal website, writing blogs, and posting photos and videos on Instagram, TikTok, and other social media platforms. Painter Josie Lewis offers this advice for marketing on social media: "I would take a look at art accounts I admire and emulate their posting style. You can glean a huge amount of information from what successful creators post, how they photograph or film their work, how often they post and how they engage with their audience."[7]

Craft artists make handmade objects that are designed to be useful as well as artistically pleasing. Woodworkers, jewelers, weavers, and potters are just a few of the craft artists who turn raw materials into items that people want and use.

Lewis says the most popular videos on her social media accounts show her working in her studio and explaining how she creates her artwork. "I really dig sharing my process on social media and over 3 million folks follow along! My art process videos have had more than 1 billion views."[8]

Education and Training

Lewis went to art school for seven years to earn two degrees: a bachelor of fine arts (BFA) and a master of fine arts. But Lewis is in the minority when it comes to educational background. The American Society of Landscape Architects says that around 42 percent of all craft artists have a bachelor's degree, while only 12 percent have a master's degree.

Whatever their educational background, most craft artists have some formal art education that taught them the necessary skills to pursue their careers. Prospective craft artists often begin their training in high school, where they take art classes, woodshop, metal shop, or home economics. These classes introduce students to working with various art materials and equipment and teach skills like drawing, painting, sculpting, woodworking, welding, and sewing. Students also commonly participate in community arts programs hosted by local art museums, organizations like the YMCA, and government programs such as the National Endowment for the Arts.

While a college education is not necessary to become a craft artist, a BFA degree can provide a solid background for those wishing to run a successful independent business. BFA programs feature courses in art history, art theory, design fundamentals, sculpture, print media, photography, digital media, and related topics. BFA students also have access to the tools and technology found in art studios, machine fabrication shops, glassblowing studios, metal foundries, woodwork shops and pottery studios.

Skills and Personality

The most obvious skill possessed by a craft artist is artistic ability coupled with a heightened sense of creativity. Many are lifelong art lovers who began drawing, painting, or making art objects at a young age. But it is not necessary to be born an artist if you are persistent. Like musicians, athletes, and even computer programmers, craft artists improve their skills through repetition. Good artists can become great artists if they have the determination to practice—and practice some more.

Most craft artists would prefer to spend their time honing their craft. But those who achieve success develop good time-management and business skills. Many artists find that the most difficult part of the job involves conducting market research, studying financial matters, and bookkeeping. Illustrator Serena Archetti writes, “Growing and running a business doesn’t usually

Selling at Art and Craft Fairs

"Selling at local events, like art markets, craft fairs, and festivals, is where I've found most of my own success as an artist. It's a tough life, to be sure, and totally exhausting at times. But it can also be really fun, meeting new people all of the time and selling your artwork in person! Selling your artwork or crafty creations in person can also be a great way to test what works and doesn't. See which themes or styles people respond to the most. Ask questions of your customers to find out what drew them into your booth."

—Mallory Whitfield, creativity marketing expert

Mallory Whitfield, "How to Make a Living as an Artist or Crafter!," Badass Creatives, May 28, 2023. www.badasscreatives.com.

come naturally for many of us, and it's often overwhelming. So, we need to be intentional and set aside time each day to focus on those tasks outside our comfort zone."[9]

Workplace Settings

Craft artists work in a variety of settings. Some rent studios in lofts, warehouses, or office buildings. Budget-minded artists might share a large studio space with other artists. Some work in home studios located in garages, basements, spare bedrooms, or outbuildings.

Wherever they work, craft artists might be exposed to hazardous materials. Sculptor Dru Perry says she stopped making stained glass windows because the job involved working with toxic lead solder. Other craft artists use glues, paints, cleaners, and a wide variety of chemicals, and these materials might require the artists to wear goggles, gloves, and breathing masks. Some crafters also work with dangerous power tools and equipment such as kilns, furnaces, and welding torches that produce extreme heat.

Successful craft artists often work more than forty hours a week, including nights and weekends. When orders come in, artists are obligated to create the products, correspond with customers, and get the goods shipped in a timely manner.

Employers and Pay

The Bureau of Labor Statistics (BLS) says that around 55 percent of all craft artists and fine artists are self-employed. Craft artists might also work for companies that produce furniture, musical instruments, kitchenware, textiles, and home decor. According to the BLS, craft artists earned a median annual income of $38,480 in 2024. However, the bureau acknowledges that income for self-employed artists can vary widely. Those who work as painters, sculptors, and illustrators earned an average of $60,560. The highest-paid 10 percent brought in more than $133,000.

What Is the Future Outlook for Craft Artists?

The BLS says employment for craft artists is expected to grow by 3 percent through 2033, about as fast as the average for all occupations. However, this projected growth depends on the economy. During periods of economic growth, people spend more on art, while spending decreases during economic downturns.

Find Out More

Alliance for California Traditional Arts (ACTA)

https://actaonline.org

The ACTA runs several apprenticeship programs for folk and traditional artists of diverse backgrounds. Apprentices receive grants, work with mentor artists, and participate in community events. The ACTA website features personal stories, newsletter, and application information.

American Craft Council (ACC)
https://craftcouncil.org
The ACC is dedicated to promoting the craft arts. The council provides craft labs, a school-to-market program, and an early career artist program. The ACC publishes the bimonthly *American Craft* magazine and hosts American Craft Shows in four cities each year.

Craft in America
www.craftinamerica.org
The organization behind the PBS documentary television series *Craft in America* operates an exhibition and learning space in Los Angeles. The group publishes education guides to support middle school and high school curricula and creates research materials and videos dedicated to craft culture and history.

What Does a Curator Do?

There are over thirty-five thousand museums in the United States—more than any other country in the world, according to the Institute of Museum and Library Services. The institutions include art, natural history, science, air and space museums, botanical gardens, nature centers, historical societies, and aquariums. Some museums are devoted to a single subject meant to attract fans with specialized interests. These places include the National Baseball Hall of Fame and Museum in Cooperstown, New York; the International UFO Museum in Roswell, New Mexico; and the San Diego Model Railroad Museum in San Diego, California. Whatever the focus of an institution, all museums have one thing in common. They are managed by curators who select, organize, and oversee museum collections.

At a Glance

Number of Jobs
14,200 in 2023

Pay
$61,770 in 2024

Educational Requirements
Bachelor's degree; master's degree is preferred

Personal Qualities
Artistic, detail oriented, analytical, good communication skills

Working Conditions
Full time with overtime in museums, offices, and exhibition openings

Future Job Outlook
Growth of 11 percent through 2033*

* For all archivists, curators, and museum workers

Curators use their extensive knowledge to acquire and exhibit collections of art and sculpture, historical objects, notable documents, and other items of interest. Curators are responsible for visualizing and creating exhibitions. These events highlight a specific subject, the work of a group of creators, or the work of a single creator. N. Elizabeth Schlatter, art curator for the University of Richmond Museums in Virginia, describes how she chooses the focus of presentations: "I think of ideas for exhibitions, usually influenced by art and artists that I see or meet or learn about. Then I work on selecting artworks that will be shown as part of the exhibition, research them, interview artists when I can, write about the art in a catalog or article, and design the layout for the exhibition."[10]

Curators are also educators. They mentor students, oversee educational programs, and conduct public tours and workshops. As Margaret A. Miller, chief curator of the University of South Florida Contemporary Art Museum, puts it, "My core value and focus is to present a program of temporary exhibitions and related educational programs that introduce students and the broader community to advanced international contemporary art."[11]

A Typical Workday

Curators spend their days communicating with others through phone calls, emails, and texts. They conduct research, fill out grant applications, and write press releases and catalog essays to promote exhibits. Curators also write the audio presentations museum visitors listen to when touring the exhibits. A big part of the job is keeping track of museum inventory and overseeing research on collection pieces. Some curators use radiocarbon dating and X-ray analysis to ensure the age and history of a piece is accurate.

Curators attend meetings with staff and supervise the work of museum archivists who authenticate and preserve artistic and historical objects. Curators meet with an array of people associated with an exhibition, which, depending on the museum, might include artists, historians, scientists, donors, educators, and other experts. Natalie Bell is a curator at a contemporary art museum, the MIT List Visual Arts Center in Massachusetts. Unlike a

An Exciting Job

"I am a curator in a really cool museum! I get to . . . . research all the artifacts in the museum, and find out lots about them and find out their history. . . . I get to touch a lot of things people wouldn't ordinarily get to touch and I think that's really exciting. Some days I am designing a new exhibition to go on show at one of the two museums I work in, that's definitely very exciting for me. And other days, I can be photographing objects that have been given to our museums. It's always very exciting when you get something new in."

—Mel Ruth Oakley, curator at Dundee Heritage Trust in the United Kingdom

Quoted in BBC Bitesize, "Working as a Curator: Mel Ruth's Story," 2025. www.bbc.co.uk.

curator at a historical museum or a science center, Bell interacts with living artists, which she says is the best part of her job. "I love working with artists and helping them bring their ideas to an audience," she asserts. "Sometimes, working with a contemporary artist means helping them realize a work in a new way that's specific to a given space. And that can be really exciting because you're bringing some sort of collaboration to the table and helping that happen."[12]

Exhibits are often on loan to museums from other cities or other countries, and curators must work with shippers to ensure that the materials are packed properly and arrive safely. When an exhibit is being set up, the curator oversees workers called exhibit fabricators. These teams of carpenters, painters, metal fabricators, and other skilled personnel pound nails, mount paintings on walls, and build displays from wood, metal, glass, plastic, and other materials. "That's the real action of the job," says Bell, "actually hanging works in the space, installing sculptures, and finding the best way to organize a given gallery space for viewers to experience and encounter the art that's on view."[13]

Education and Training

Curators are acknowledged authorities in their field who have a strong educational background in the subjects they curate. Small museums might require applicants to have at least a bachelor's degree in art education, marketing, business administration, or related subjects. However, most major museums require curators to have at least a master's degree in art history, history, archaeology, zoology, or museum studies. Curating is a very competitive field, and those who possess a PhD have a better chance of finding work, especially at large or renowned institutions.

Prospective curators can start in high school by learning as much as possible about their favorite topic. Individuals who hope to become curators at a natural history museum, for example, would immerse themselves in subjects like geology, biology, and zoology. John R. Demboski, chief curator at the Denver Museum of Nature & Science, developed a love of museums as a teenager after volunteering at the Cincinnati Museum of Natural History. As a college student he conducted fieldwork studying large mammals and evolution. With a PhD in zoology, Demboski manages a team of scientists, oversees exhibitions and collections, and develops educational programming.

Many curators begin their careers as curatorial assistants or collection managers when they are still in graduate school. Those who move up the career ladder work as curatorial associates who oversee interns and volunteers, draw up budget documents, and assist in the procurement of art collections from donors and others.

Skills and Personality

Curators are lifelong learners who take every opportunity to enhance their knowledge. As Schlatter says, "Like a lot of people who have the joy of working in the field of their passion, I . . . spend a good portion of my free time doing things related to my job, like

A curator and staff member prepare for a new art exhibit. In addition to creating exhibitions, curators select, organize, and oversee collections of art, historical objects, notable documents, and more for museums and galleries.

visiting other museums and galleries, reading about art online or in publications, and writing or curating projects as freelance."[14]

Curators use analytical skills to delve into the history, significance, and cultural relevance of the objects they work with. And they are detail oriented and able to remember key features of the artifacts held in storage by their institutions. Curators also need what are called soft skills or people skills. Whether they are engaging with the public or museum staff, they need to be able to communicate effectively, work collaboratively, and maintain a positive attitude when problems arise. Foreign language skills are a plus for those who work with historical art and other objects.

Many curators find themselves following their childhood dreams. Jacqueline Goldstein spent most of her career curating

Making a Meaningful Impact on Visitors

"*Relative Truths* is a selection of artwork created by the faculty of the University of Utah Department of Art & Art History. . . . My role in this exhibition was to carefully select the artwork which I found to be most critically engaged or contributed to a greater and cohesive whole of an exhibition and do my best to provide . . . information that might help the visitor glean more meaning from their experience visiting the gallery. In a way, being a curator . . . [is] to be a thoughtful liaison of sorts between artist and institution and artwork and museum visitor."

—Peter Hay, visual arts manager at the Utah Division of Arts & Museums

Quoted in J. Attridge, "Curator Interview: Peter Hay," *At the Heart of It All* (blog), Utah Museum of Fine Arts. https://umfa.utah.edu.

art exhibitions. But she always loved fast cars, which led her to become the curator of the San Diego Automotive Museum in 2025. Goldstein says, "[I] have always been in the art world, but cars have always been my love. I learned to drive . . . with my dad when I was a kid . . . and it's a dream job to be working with cars all day." Goldstein says the best part of her job is passing her knowledge on to the public during curator tours. "They learn that a car might not just be cool but it's fast. And we can talk about why it's fast. We can also talk about car culture and the artistry of cars and how it relates to design."[15]

Workplace Settings

Curators work full time in offices and museum buildings. They also work nights and weekends when their institutions hold exhibitions, opening receptions, or fundraising events with donors. Curators sometimes work odd hours when museums are not open to the public. Travel is required for those conducting fieldwork and obtaining items from distant locations.

Employers and Pay

Curators work in museums, art galleries, educational institutions, religious organizations, and government agencies. Some curators work in teams with other specialists. For example, the Whitney Museum of American Art in New York City has a photography curator, a Latin American art curator, and a sculpture curator. Like other large museums, the Whitney also hires freelance curators for special exhibitions.

The Whitney is privately owned and funded, like most museums in the United States. But there are well-known national museums that are funded by the federal government. The most prominent are part of the Smithsonian Institution in Washington, DC. These include the American Art Museum, the National Air and Space Museum, and the National Museum of African American History and Culture.

The Bureau of Labor Statistics (BLS) says curators earned a median income of $61,770 in 2024. The lowest-paid 10 percent of earners made under $35,000, while the highest-paid 10 percent brought in more than $98,000.

What Is the Future Outlook for Curators?

The BLS says that job opportunities for curators are expected to grow by 11 percent through 2033, much faster than the average for all occupations. According to the bureau, this growth will be fueled by the need to replace workers who transfer to other occupations or retire. As long as museums continue to attract the public, curators will be needed to oversee collections.

Find Out More

American Alliance of Museums

www.aam-us.org

The alliance is one of the main resources for museum employees, including curators and archivists. Its website offers a jobs board, videos focused on museum education, and access to blogs, books, and *Museum* magazine.

Association of Art Museum Curators (AAMC)

www.artcurators.org

The AAMC is an organization for curators of art museums that offers webinars, a jobs board, conferences, and professional development programs. The association supports professionals in the field and educates the public about the important role curators play in preserving history and culture.

Center for Curatorial Leadership (CCL)

www.curatorialleadership.org

The CCL is dedicated to training art curators to become visionary leaders by providing supportive publications, fellowship opportunities, and seminars. The center also offers a mentorship program and other educational projects focused on museum challenges and strategies.

Music Director

What Does a Music Director Do?

In the world of classical music, Gustavo Dudamel is a superstar. Dudamel, born in Venezuela in 1981, is the son of a trombonist and a voice teacher. He began studying music when he was five years old, learned to play violin at age eleven, and first conducted the Venezuela national youth orchestra, officially called the Simón Bolívar Symphony Orchestra, when he was fifteen. In 2007, when he was twenty-six, Dudamel was appointed music director of the Los Angeles Philharmonic, a job he held until 2025. In this role Dudamel led the Los Angeles Philharmonic and selected compositions for the one-hundred-member orchestra to perform live and on recordings.

> ### At a Glance
>
> **Number of Jobs**
> 50,300 in 2023
>
> **Pay**
> $63,670 in 2024
>
> **Educational Requirements**
> Bachelor's degree in music
>
> **Personal Qualities**
> Musical talent, perseverance, discipline, good communicator
>
> **Working Conditions**
> Full time in studios, rehearsal spaces, and concert venues; travel required
>
> **Future Job Outlook**
> Growth of 3 percent through 2033

Music directors are commonly referred to as conductors. Those who work in this music profession stand before an orchestra on a podium that holds a complete musical score. Using a baton, hand gestures, and facial expressions, the conductor sets the rhythm and tempo (speed) of the music. Music directors cue various orchestra sections to start and stop playing, and they control dynamics (volume levels) of the music. Without their guidance individual musicians would start playing at different times, creating musical chaos. Most well-known conductors are also compelling to watch as they engage audiences with their style and flair. Classical music journalist Joshua Barone describes Dudamel's talent for entertaining: "If Gustavo Dudamel . . . is known for anything, it's the sheer energy of his performances. His body moves with dancerly charisma as his baton conjures extremities of orchestral sound; the music feels alive, and so do you."[16]

Most music directors never reach the level of fame achieved by Dudamel, but they play a central role in directing the music played by orchestras, choirs, and other ensembles. Music directors conduct rehearsals in which they critique the overall presentation and the performance of individual musicians. Music directors audition and hire new musicians, enlist guest performers, and choose soloists. They are also the public face of an orchestra. Music directors give interviews to reporters, meet with donors, and appear at fundraisers.

Respect, Guide, and Inspire

"Take the time to learn and to develop your ideas as an artist. Competitions should be seen as an opportunity to gain experience and learn from others. The most important thing is to respect the musicians in the orchestra. You have to respect their tradition, and you learn to balance in the moment. Music has an immediate reaction that you have to be aware of. Everything can change, and you must be flexible. Conducting is psychological, and you have to inspire and guide. . . . For conductors, it's all about understanding the dynamic of creating an interpretation with others."

—Gustavo Dudamel, music and artistic director of the Los Angeles Philharmonic

Quoted in John Knight, "An Interview with Gustavo Dudamel," *The Instrumentalist*, 2024. https://theinstrumentalist.com.

Some music directors compose original music for orchestras, musical plays, and movies. Renowned twentieth-century music director Leonard Bernstein composed three symphonies as well as the score to the musical *West Side Story*. Music director John Williams wrote some of the most famous film scores in movie history, including the themes from *Star Wars*, *Harry Potter and the Philosopher's Stone*, and all the films in the *Indiana Jones* franchise.

A Typical Workday

Music director Kyle Mattingly says there is no typical workday in his job: "There really isn't a normal day for us musicians. Every day has a different puzzle to figure out. As a composer/arranger, most of the time you're trying to figure out what a client needs for their project and how to adapt the music to fit that goal."[17]

Mattingly says individual musicians can play whatever inspires them. But music directors must devise programs that will attract attention and draw in the public. They also need to collaborate with musicians and the boards of directors that own and operate most orchestras. Music directors use various tools to perform this work. They might develop programs using synthesizers or digital audio software that allow them to experiment with different sounds and pieces of music. They develop ideas by listening to a wide array of music from classical to pop and even rap and country. Playwright, actor, and music director Lin-Manuel Miranda famously linked hip hop lyrics with orchestral music for his award-winning musical *Hamilton*.

After selecting pieces for a program, a music director will write out musical scores by hand, create them using software, or obtain published scores. Music directors might play pieces on a piano or other instruments and tweak the scores to give them a unique sound. Arrangements for individual players or sections of the orchestra might be rewritten. When scores are completed, music directors present them to musicians, who rehearse on a weekly or monthly schedule, depending on upcoming programs.

As with many other occupations, music directors have to perform administrative tasks. They organize rehearsal schedules, manage budgets, approve contracts, and communicate with musicians, assistants, patrons, stage managers, and others by email, text, and telephone. Some, like Dudamel, who manage famous orchestras, oversee assistants responsible for administrative tasks.

Education and Training

Most conductors study music and learn to play musical instruments at an early age. As Dudamel says, "I think every child has a natural talent for music, every young person can play an instrument, learn to sing, and dance. Maybe it leads to a career, maybe it becomes a lifelong passion alongside other things; the point is that the gift of music is for everyone, not just for those like me."[18]

Students can enjoy the gift of music by playing in ensembles or singing in choirs at school, religious institutions, or community centers. Students also study individually with music teachers and mentors. Additionally, students can take workshops offered by associations such as the League of American Orchestras and the Conductors Guild or on websites like Musical Chairs. These programs can be expensive, but according to Diane Wittry, the music director of the Allentown Symphony Orchestra, "[Think of it as] an investment in yourself and your career."[19]

Like many accomplished classical musicians, Dudamel entered (and won) many youth music competitions. At the time most competitions were live, but today musicians can participate in online contests like the International Youth Music Competitions.

College students who wish to compose and become music directors typically choose one of two degree paths. They either pursue a bachelor of music degree or a bachelor of fine arts in music degree. Students pursuing music degrees also need to play

Los Angeles Philharmonic music director and conductor Gustavo Dudamel pauses to acknowledge the audience after a performance. Dudamel held his position with the orchestra from 2007 to 2025.

in orchestras, according to Raphael Jiménez, director of orchestras at Oberlin College and Conservatory. "You should definitely be a strong performer and get as much performing experience as possible; so an undergraduate degree in performance is recommended," he says. "If you have a strong interest in conducting as an undergraduate, you should take courses in orchestration and composition."[20] Other studies might include music in culture, music and the media, and the relationship between music and wellness.

Choir directors do not often need a graduate degree, but most organizations that hire conductors or classical music composers prefer candidates that hold either a master of music or master of arts in music. Some schools offer a master of music in music conducting. Graduate-level courses teach the philosophy of music education, theories of rhythm and meter, conducting techniques, orchestration, and music technology.

Skills and Personality

Those who wish to be music directors need to be extremely dedicated and focused. It might be a cliché to say musicians need to practice, practice, practice, but this is especially true for conductors. Conducting is a physical skill as well as a musical skill. Those who succeed are extremely disciplined when it comes to developing their talents. They spend many hours a day focused on improving their conducting skills and playing techniques.

Succeeding as a music director requires perseverance. Rejection is part of the game, and music directors seeking employment have to learn to deal with disappointment.

Music directors are excellent communicators. As leaders of orchestras or choirs, they need to provide guidance and support to musicians in a personable manner. Music directors also use their communication skills when promoting their organizations to community groups, to students, and on social media.

Workplace Settings

Music directors may work in offices, recording studios, rehearsal halls, classrooms, orchestra halls, and other entertainment venues. They work full time but seldom keep the traditional nine-to-five business hours, since performances are usually held in the evenings, on weekends, and during holidays. Music directors often travel to give lectures and seminars and to conduct in venues around the globe.

Employers and Pay

Music directors lead a variety of musical ensembles, including church choirs, opera companies, youth orchestras, theater orchestras, and high school and college orchestras. Some oversee educational programs meant to inspire young people to listen to and play classical music. Music directors are most often

> **Start Composing Now**
>
> "[Most composers] are working with a group, company, or another artist and trying to fit their music into a bigger goal. This means that some days you're figuring out how to write music for a choir and the next might be programming synth sounds to sound like a big movie trailer. . . . If you like those things, start trying to do some of that work now. You can find a song or project and try to write/arrange something that would fit it. You'll get better and continue to learn along the way. That's exactly how the big guys started."
>
> —Kyle Mattingly, part-time music director at Walt Disney World
>
> Kyle Mattingly, "What Is a Typical Day Like as a Music Composer/Arranger?," CareerVillage.org, May 31, 2022. www.careervillage.org.

employed by organizations that produce live performances, including music, theater, and dance companies. Some work for religious organizations or educational institutions. The Bureau of Labor Statistics (BLS) says the median annual wage for music directors was $63,670 in 2024. Those who worked for performing arts companies earned an average of $75,040, while music directors working for religious organizations brought in $60,510 on average. Prestigious conductors like Dudamel can command salaries of millions of dollars.

What Is the Future Outlook for Music Directors?

The BLS says employment of music directors and composers is expected to grow by 3 percent through 2033, about as fast as the average for all occupations. Most music groups rely on donations, corporate sponsorships, and ticket sales, however. This leads the BLS to say that employment for music directors might not grow at the expected figure if money diminishes due to government and corporate budget cuts or economic downturns.

Find Out More

American Choral Directors Association (ACDA)

https://acda.org

The ACDA promotes choral music through competitions, education, and performance. The association has programs for composers, K–12 choral educators, and students. Its website features blogs and a daily newsletter.

International Youth Music Competitions

www.internationalyouthmusiccompetitions.org

This organization stages monthly online music competitions in several genres for young musicians of different skill levels. Performances are critiqued by judges, and prizes are awarded. Winners go on to compete in a winner's recital in New York City.

National Association of Schools of Music (NASM)

https://nasm.arts-accredit.org

The NASM is an internationally recognized accreditation organization for music schools in the United States. Its website provides information about postsecondary degree programs in music.

What Does an Interior Designer Do?

Interior designers shape indoor environments so that they are comfortable, functional, safe, and beautiful. To do so, these professionals rely on a combination of creativity, an eye for detail, and good problem-solving skills. Interior designers choose colors, fabrics, and textiles for walls, carpets, and furniture. They make rooms unique with the placement of decorative objects, like lamps, paintings, and figurines. The work of interior designers can be seen in restaurants, lounges, executive office suites, and the homes of rich and not-so-rich clients. C.T. Nguyen, chair of Interior Design at the Savannah College of Art and Design, describes the job: "An interior designer creates art that humans literally live, work, and play within."[21]

At a Glance

Number of Jobs
92,200 in 2023

Pay
$63,490 in 2024

Educational Requirements
Bachelor's degree

Personal Qualities
Artistic, math and computer design skills, business sense, good communicator

Working Conditions
In offices at computers and drafting tables, forty-plus hours a week; some travel to homes of clients

Future Job Outlook
Growth of 4 percent through 2033

Creating inhabitable art requires interior designers to have a good grasp of design history and architecture. Most bring their ideas to life using design software like Autodesk Revit and HomeByMe. Interior designers also need to be good project managers. They must create and follow budgets and timelines and work smoothly with construction crews and artisans, like furniture makers and drapery

Be Your Own Social Media Manager

"I manage my own social media, however, it's very time consuming and it's not easy. . . . You're doing multiple jobs such as content strategy, where you have to come up with different ways to be creating so that you can develop and implement new ideas. Customer relations and response, engaging with my supporters. . . . You'll also have to educate yourself on how the algorithm works. Each day has a different time to post. So it's important that you learn how the algorithm operates so that your posts will be seen when the apps are being used the most."

—Tiffany Clark, interior designer

Quoted in CanvasRebel, "Meet Tiffany Clark Interior Designer," August 19, 2024. https://canvasrebel.com.

seamstresses. And interior designers need a good understanding of building codes to ensure that plumbing, electrical, and structural systems are safe and secure. For new structures and major renovations, interior designers might be involved in construction. Designer Joan Kaufman explains, "There is the aspect of picking out paint and pillows—my firm does that too—but we can also gut a bathroom and draw up our own blueprints."[22]

Beyond their technical and creative expertise, interior designers thrive in a tough, competitive business. Finding new clients is an interior designer's number one business challenge. Most interior designers promote their work, establish themselves as experts, and attract new clients by maintaining an up-to-date presence on social media. This involves creating digital portfolios on personal websites and posting content to TikTok, Instagram, Facebook, Pinterest, and other platforms. Those who take the time and effort to promote themselves effectively can find success. Interior designer Tiffany Clark says that 95 percent of her business comes from the work she puts into her social media accounts: "When I first started out it was a way for me to save money. . . . My online audience grew overnight with organic followers and comments. Being consistent with good quality videos and posting at the right time really does make a difference."[23]

Some of the most successful interior designers use their prominence to launch their own brands. Bobby Berk, who starred as the interior designer expert on the Netflix series *Queer Eye*, went on to create his own lines of furniture, art, and wallpaper.

A Typical Workday

Interior designers work closely with clients, contractors, and vendors, which means most days are filled with phone calls, texts, emails, and virtual meetings on platforms like Zoom, Slack, and Google Meet. Face-to-face meetings and site visits are also central to the job. During meetings interior designers take notes and make informal sketches. After a meeting ends, the designer will conduct research to match colors and materials with the client's aspirations and visions. When this work is completed, designers will sit down at a computer and create numerous digital pictures of proposed room designs.

Interior designers are increasingly using virtual reality (VR) headsets to provide clients with an immersive experience so that they can feel what it is like to "walk" through high-quality 3-D digital renderings of the rooms the designers have in mind. Clients can look at rooms from different angles, request alternate views, and get an idea of the scale and proportions of a room. Interior designer Luis Carmona writes, "VR empowers designers to create extraordinary spaces while ensuring client satisfaction. By leveraging virtual reality, designers can step into their designs long before they become a physical reality, enhancing creativity, efficiency, and the overall design outcome."[24]

Keeping up with social media can be a big job, and designers often spend around 20 percent of their day or more posting high-quality images, illustrations, and other content to their portfolios

An interior designer discusses color options with her clients. To achieve the look their clients want—whether for a home or business—interior designers consider colors, fabrics, and textiles for walls, carpets, and furniture.

and websites. Some interior designers share their artistic visions and creative thoughts on blogs, which can help attract clients from around the world. Blogs can also be money earners when they are used to promote sponsored content. Interior designer Sabina Brandonisio writes, "Overall, an interior design blog can be a powerful tool for designers to showcase their work, connect with potential clients, and establish themselves as thought leaders in the industry."[25]

Education and Training

Some interior designers, like Berk, are self-taught, but most firms that hire interior designers require job candidates to have a degree such as a bachelor of fine arts in interior design or a bachelor of science in interior design. Most colleges and universities offer interior design programs through their art, architecture, or design departments. Degree programs focus on design, textiles, color theory, design history, and 3-D modeling. All degree programs in interior design are accredited by the Council for Interior Design Accreditation or the National Association of Schools of Art and Design.

The curriculum of an interior design program focuses on both the artistic and practical aspects of the profession. Students learn aesthetics such as visual design, lighting design, art and architectural history, and the psychology of color. Courses that deal with the practical aspect of interior design focus on sustainable design and computer-aided design.

Interior design programs also emphasize public safety. Several courses focus on building codes and regulations that govern indoor air quality, lighting safety, and other aspects of construction. Interior designers also have to understand a complex array of safety issues, such as the types of flooring materials that are slip resistant and what types of materials emit toxic compounds that create indoor air pollution. Fire safety courses emphasize the importance of obvious features like fire alarms and ceiling sprinklers. But fire codes extend to regulations that determine appropriate lengths, widths, and clearances of aisles and doorways in case a building needs to be evacuated during an emergency. Flammable materials such as wood, textiles, and carpet are required to comply with fire resistance ratings issued by the National Fire Protection Association.

After graduation, those who want to improve their job prospects can become certified by the Council for Interior Design Qualification. Similarly, interior designers who specialize in kitchens and bathrooms obtain certification from the National Kitchen and Bath Association. Depending on the certification, an interior designer may be able to use formal job titles such as commercial interior designer, residential interior designer, or lighting designer.

Skills and Personality

Interior designers are artistic and creative professionals who translate their visions of beauty into practical systems through drawings, computer programs, and business skills. They need to understand math to take precise measurements of rooms that can be accurately translated into purchase orders and blueprints. Interior designers also use math when they negotiate contracts with clients, builders, plumbers, electricians, and suppliers. They need to ensure that budgets are followed and deadlines are met.

An interior designer needs to be customer focused and flexible to work smoothly with clients who can be difficult. Living spaces are intimate and private, which means clients can be justifiably fussy. Some clients have a clear understanding about what they want, while others might choose decor that they end up hating when the room is finished. Interior designer Carmen Brown counsels those in her field to learn to go with the flow: "Rarely ever does everything go to plan exactly how it's supposed to no matter how organized of a planner you are. Expect delays, mistakes, minds changing, and disappointments."[26]

Workplace Settings

Interior designers work in offices at computers and drafting tables. Most interior designers work at least forty hours a week, but the job sometimes requires long hours when deadlines are looming. Interior designers often travel to homes, businesses, and other establishments to meet customers, conduct research, and oversee construction.

Employers and Pay

Around one-third of interior designers work at design firms, while 20 percent are self-employed. Others work for architectural or engineering firms or furniture stores. The Bureau of Labor Statistics (BLS) says interior designers earned an annual median salary of

Expensive but Worth It

"It's not always as glamorous as it looks from the outside. Running an Interior Design business is 90% business, and 10% design. Definitely not something I realized when I started this journey. There are bookkeepers, program fees, contractors who draw CAD [computer-aided design] and more technical things I don't do (or like to do for that matter). . . . It's an expensive (and busy) business to run, but I also know the return is so worth it for me because at the end of the day, I get to help people . . . experience the joy and serenity that I feel in my own home."

—Jenna Maenhout, interior designer

Jenna Maenhout, "How I Got into Interior Design," Styled Out West, March 8, 2023. www.styledoutwest.com.

$63,490 in 2024. The highest-paid 10 percent of earners brought in more than $106,090.

What Is the Future Outlook for Interior Designers?

The BLS says that employment for interior designers is expected to grow by 4 percent through 2033. However, those who specialize in environmentally friendly designs or designs for easier accessibility will be in higher demand. And because there will always be clients interested in unique personal spaces in homes and offices, the demand for services by experienced interior designers will remain strong.

Find Out More

American Society of Interior Designers (ASID)

www.asid.org

The American Society of Interior Designers supports the interior design profession through education, advocacy, and community outreach. ASID provides student grants and scholarships, hosts a student portfolio competition, and features a job bank where students can find career advice and post their résumés.

Council for Interior Design Accreditation (CIDA)
https://cida.org
The CIDA provides accreditation for interior design programs at colleges and universities in most states and in Canada. Prospective interior designers can find information on the council's website about academic programs, licensing requirements, and life as a professional in the field.

Council for Interior Design Qualification (CIDQ)
www.cidq.org
The CIDQ administers the nationally recognized NCIDQ certification exam that interior designers are required to pass to be registered and licensed in many states. Students interested in interior design can find numerous details about the profession and certification requirements on the council's website.

National Association of Schools of Arts and Design (NASAD)
https://nasad.arts-accredit.org
The NASAD has established national standards for undergraduate and graduate degrees in art and design. Students wishing to pursue an art degree from high-quality institutions can select from more than 360 accredited art schools, colleges, conservatories, and universities listed on the NASAD website.

Landscape Designer

What Does a Landscape Designer Do?

Rochelle Greayer worked on projects in outer space before she found her ideal career digging in the ground as a landscape designer. Greayer earned a degree in applied physics and landed a job designing communications satellites. After she was laid off from her job, Greayer attended a large flower show. The auditorium was filled with displays of elaborate floral arrangements and prize-winning plants and flowers. As Greayer tells it, the flower show changed her life: "I was amazed by the gardens and feats of horticulture. . . . I had never considered that there was any garden-related industry—let alone one so glamorous and exciting. The show brought together landscape design, horticulture, business, entrepreneurship, and media through gardens."[27] Greayer soon launched her own business. As a landscape designer, she was able to combine her design skills, her scientific understanding of the natural world, and her love of plants.

At a Glance

Number of Jobs
24,000 in 2023

Pay
$70,371 in 2025

Educational Requirements
None, but a bachelor's degree is recommended

Personal Qualities
Artistic, knowledge of plants and biology, computer design skills, good communicator, business acumen

Working Conditions
Full time with some overtime on weekends; in offices and outdoor spaces, sometimes in inclement weather

Future Job Outlook
Growth of 5 percent through 2033*

* For all landscape architects

Few landscape designers are former physicists. What most landscape designers have in common, however, is an eye for beauty and an extensive knowledge of plants, including shrubs, trees, and flowers. Landscape designers create plans for gardens, walkways, fountains, outdoor lighting, and other features. They oversee the installation of gardens in residential yards, public parks, playgrounds, golf courses, college campuses, and shopping centers. Landscape designers work with homeowners, corporate clients, urban planners, park supervisors, and public agencies.

The landscape designer's artistic canvas is the natural world in both rural and urban areas—any place where people interact with the environment. When designing landscapes, these professionals rely on a broad range of talents and technical skills. Some landscape designers use colored pencils, watercolors, and acrylic paint to create detailed drawings, diagrams, and plans for gardens. Designers also work on computers using 2-D and 3-D outdoor design software apps, including AutoCAD LT, PRO Landscape, and Vectorworks Landmark. Landscape designers must also be skillful at promoting their work in local garden stores and on social media. And they need the financial skills to take care of business and accounting tasks.

One of the fastest-growing trends in landscape design is environmental sustainability. Professionals in this eco-friendly field emphasize the use of native plants while shunning pesticides, herbicides, and other agricultural chemicals. Sustainable landscape designers work to preserve the natural environment, improve air and water quality, and conserve power, among other objectives. To attain these goals, they use recycled construction materials and promote the use of rainwater harvesting systems and solar panels.

Some landscape designers have achieved a level of fame for their work. Landscape designer Mike Pyle cohosts the HGTV show *Inside Out*, on which he pitches his design plans to clients while carefully striving to stay within set budgets. Vickie Cardaro is a nationally recognized landscape designer whose work has been featured in *Architectural Digest* and other publications.

How I Got Started

"I recommend reaching out to a local landscape designer and ask them about their work and how they got there. You might even be able to [get] some work experience with them which would be valuable. Other advice I would give is to get a casual job at your local nursery. That's where I began. During my studies this casual job helped me to develop my passion and knowledge of plants. Finally, start drawing! Everyone can draw no matter what. The key is to start. Hand drawing is one of the foundational skills needed before moving on to the CAD programs and becoming a well-rounded landscape designer."

—Ben Miura, landscape designer

Quoted in Donnay Torr, "A Day in the Life of . . . a Landscape Designer," Skills Road, 2025. https://skillsroad.com.

Some landscape designers go on to become landscape architects. In addition to designing gardens, landscape architects are qualified to draw up plans for stairways, walls, sidewalks, large water features, and other structures known as hardscape. Landscape architects most often design outdoor features for major projects like shopping centers, school campuses, office developments, and public parks. They work with surveyors, engineers, environmental researchers, and building architects.

A Typical Workday

While Greayer was struck by the allure of the flower show, most landscape designers are not attracted to the profession for the glamour or glory. On any given day, landscape designers can be found at garden stores hauling plants and bags of mulch. They toil outdoors in inclement weather and dig up weeds in the hot sun while dodging stinging bugs, thorns, and poison ivy. But before any of that work can commence, landscape designers spend their days planning a project.

Design tasks take place in a home office or office suite, where the designer meets with new clients to learn what they want. When a new project gets started, the designer needs to ask questions. How much time does the client spend in the yard? What are the client's favorite colors and plants? How big is the space, and is it sunny or shady? How much money does the client want to invest in the project? Do they want a low-maintenance yard or a yard that requires a great deal of care?

During the initial process, landscape designers visit the proposed site, where they take detailed measurements of lot elevation, width, and length. With this information, the designer might create three or more different designs for a client, each one at a different estimated price. The plans generally feature a combination of hand-drawn sketches and conceptual designs created on a computer with landscape design software. The plans help a client visualize three-dimensional spaces, color-coordinated gardens, fountains, walkways, and other features. Most plans also feature time projections to help a client see what a space will look like in five to ten years. When plans are completed, the landscape designer will meet with the client to provide price quotes, discuss changes, and settle on project completion dates.

Before work begins, the designer will conduct a thorough analysis of the site. Soil samples are sent to a soil biologist to determine the texture, density, nutrients, and presence of organic matter. With this knowledge, the landscape designer can prepare the soil to ensure that the new plants will thrive. Landscape designers working on-site also examine drainage and other environmental characteristics that will impact the site. As landscape designer Angelica Diaz explains, "Site analysis is more than just understanding the immediate environment. It's about considering the broader context, including the surrounding neighborhood and city. This helps identify the project's needs and how . . . we can create a beautiful and sustainable space."[28]

Landscape designers must have an eye for beauty and an extensive knowledge of all types of plants. In addition to choosing the right plants for each project, they develop plans for gardens, walkways, fountains, outdoor lighting, and other features.

Once the project moves to the implementation phase, the landscape designer will adjust cost estimates, create a project plan, and hire workers. As the project takes shape, the landscape designer acts as a project manager, visiting the site regularly and ensuring that the plans are being executed properly. Once the project is complete, most landscape designers remain in touch with their clients and might return to the site to make sure plants are thriving and the landscape is maturing as planned.

Education and Training

Some landscape designers choose their careers because they grew up loving both art and plants. As landscape designer Ben Miura says, "I would encourage any young person who has a passion for design and nature to pursue a career in Landscape Design."[29]

In many states, eager individuals can become landscape designers simply by printing up business cards and finding clients to pay them for the work. However, those who complete a bachelor of science in landscape architecture can stand out from the

An Affection for the Outdoors and a Grasp of Good Design Principles

"I think one of the most important things a person must have before embarking on a career in garden design is a deep love for the outdoors, no matter what the weather. The work can be brutally hard, cold, and filthy—it isn't at all glamorous most of the time. It's a complicated job which requires many different skills and disciplines to do well. One must have an understanding of good design principles, construction, drainage, soil, as well as a firm grasp on site specific growing conditions and plant suitability. This all might sound daunting and even a bit terrifying but it's what makes the job rewarding and interesting."

—Butter Wakefield, landscape designer

Quoted in Eleanor Cording-Booth, "What It's Really Like to Be a Garden Designer and How to Get There," *House & Garden*, May 17, 2024. www.houseandgarden.co.uk.

competition and land more prestigious projects. College programs focus on basic design principles, horticulture (growing ornamental plants), environmental stewardship, and professional practices.

Degree programs also highlight STEM topics—science, technology, engineering, and math. For instance, designers must understand botany, biology, geology, chemistry, and environmental sciences to grasp how plants grow and thrive in specific spaces. And math is essential for learning fundamental geometric concepts. As mathematics blogger Roslyn explains, "Geometry is the branch of mathematics that deals with the study of shapes, sizes, and positions of objects. . . . Geometric principles are used to analyze the site, measure its dimensions, and create accurate plans and designs."[30]

Landscape designers who complete their college courses wind up with dynamic portfolios that they can use to promote themselves and obtain work. Portfolios feature drawings, plans, letters of recommendation, and photos of completed projects. Recent graduates sometimes jump-start their careers by joining a garden club, volunteering to work with an established landscape designer, or doing some free gardening work for a relative or neighbor.

Skills and Personality

Many professionals in the field are proficient artists, horticulturists, and digital designers. Landscape designers generate business by showcasing their talents and convincing clients to hire them, which requires good communication and people skills. They utilize their business and management skills to set budgets, meet deadlines, and implement and oversee projects.

Workplace Settings

Landscape artists work full time in offices and in outdoor settings, sometimes in rain or extreme heat or cold. When projects are underway, they might work overtime, meeting with clients at jobsites on weekends. Most are not afraid to get their hands dirty when performing tasks like taking soil samples and planting trees, shrubs, or flowers. Sometimes they must wear protective gear like hard hats, goggles, and gloves if a job requires construction or demolition.

Employers and Pay

Around one-quarter of landscape designers are self-employed. Those who do not run their own business might work for government agencies like park departments or for architectural and outdoor design companies. The employment website ZipRecruiter says landscape designers earned an average annual wage of $70,371 in 2025.

What Is the Future Outlook for Landscape Designers?

The Bureau of Labor Statistics (BLS) does not cite figures for landscape designers, but it does reference landscape architects, the licensed professionals who tend to focus on larger projects. The BLS expects the demand for landscape architects to grow by 5 percent through 2023, slightly faster than the average. Landscape designer Scott McLeod believes the demand for landscape designers will grow at a similar rate if not faster. “As urban areas continue to grow, the demand for sustainable and aesthetically pleasing outdoor spaces is on the rise. This means more opportunities for landscape designers to showcase their creativity and technical skills,”[31] McLeod says.

Find Out More

American Society of Landscape Architects (ASLA)
www.asla.org
The ASLA is the national professional association for landscape architects and has seventy-two student chapters throughout the country. The organization offers online learning and scholarships and provides general information about starting a career.

Association of Professional Landscape Designers (APLD)
www.apld.org
The APLD is dedicated to promoting landscape designers as qualified professionals. Its website offers an online certification program, confers landscape design awards, and posts a jobs board.

National Association of Landscape Professionals (NALP)
www.landscapeprofessionals.org
The NALP is focused on advancing the profession of landscape design through education, training, and advocacy. Its website offers scholarships and educational information on horticulture, business, and sustainability. Community programs focus on young professionals, Latinos, and women.

Video Game Designer

What Does a Video Game Designer Do?

Mortal Kombat is one of the most successful video games in history. It has sold over 100 million copies and generated a media franchise that includes comic books, novels, animated TV shows, and a live-action tour. Millions of people around the world are familiar with *Mortal Kombat* and its sequels, but far fewer can name John Tobias, the video game designer who cocreated the original game. Born in 1969, Tobias took art classes in high school and began drawing comic books. Inspired by steadily improving video game graphics in the early 1990s, Tobias decided to become a video game designer. He created *Mortal Kombat*'s settings, themes, and storylines, along with the game's iconic characters, including Liu Kang, Goro, and Scorpion. In 2012, on the twentieth anniversary of *Mortal Kombat*'s release, Tobias recalled his early days as a game designer: "When we were working on [the first *Mortal Kombat*] our focus was on the game itself. Ideas of sequels or [secondary] successes weren't even a part of the thought process. Although, when creating the fiction, I had grand thoughts of a vast universe that I wasn't sure I'd have a chance to explore outside of the original game."[32]

At a Glance

Number of Jobs
127,846 in 2025

Pay
$149,118 in 2025

Educational Requirements
Bachelor's degree

Personal Qualities
Art skills, technical proficiency, perfectionist, patient, good communicator

Working Conditions
Full time in offices and studios; a lot of overtime but generally flexible hours

Future Job Outlook
Growth of 12 percent through 2030

Few job descriptions require having what Tobias calls "grand thoughts of a vast universe," but the ability to think grandly while creating new worlds and distant universes is an essential job requirement for those who design video games. Video games are deeply rooted in modern culture, and those who design them need to draw on an extraordinary level of creative talent to appeal to the game-playing public. Game designers also need highly developed technical skills that can be used to continually push the medium to new levels of design, speed, and entertainment value.

Video game designers combine their game-playing enthusiasm with the skills necessary to visualize and implement video game mechanics. They invent game concepts, maps, characters, stories, and settings that can be applied to different gaming platforms ranging from simple apps to immersive virtual reality environments. Game designers often work as part of a team when bringing basic game concepts to life. Corporate video game designers also work with programmers, artists, sound designers, and other technical staff. Their team will include production people who decide on the game's target audience while drawing up schedules and budgets.

Video game designers often specialize in a single aspect of game production. Content designers work on games before they are produced, creating a game's overall plot, characters, and settings. While content designers can let their imaginations run wild, they must stick to cohesive themes. For example, if a game takes place in medieval times, the content designer must be sure not to include things that might not be of the era, such as a machine gun or a Roman chariot.

Game mechanics designers, also called gameplay designers, focus on the rules of a game and what is called the balance or fairness of the game. Some mechanics designers create games in which everyone has a chance to win. Other games reward those with the highest skill levels. Level designers, also called environmental designers, create fantasy or realistic environments and fashion

> ### Focus on the Fun
>
> "As a game designer, you first and foremost need to be a master of HOW to make a game or level FUN, interesting, compelling, and something a player would want to play. If you are just getting started, you need to focus on how to find and design the fun over learning how to create art from scratch, how to program in C, or do any of the other thousand jobs that are needed to make a great game. Stay focused and realize that game design requires you to be a lifelong learner. You cannot learn it all this year, and maybe not in a lifetime."
>
> —Troy Dunniway, head of game design at CG Spectrum
>
> Troy Dunniway, "What Skills Do You Need as a Video Game Designer?," CG Spectrum, 2024. www.cgspectrum.com.

characters and objects that inhabit each playing level of the game. Game designer Alexander Brazie explains, "A video game level designer combines the art, systems and gameplay features together to create the spaces, obstacles and objectives of the game world called game levels. . . . Level designers are responsible for ensuring that the game's final vision is consistent, clear and compelling."[33]

Lead game designers oversee the entire game-production operation. They take sketches and ideas from content designers and turn them into playable games. Lead game designers create concise documentation for every aspect of the game, including locations, characters, rules, objects, and playing modes. The lead designer coordinates with artists, programmers, and other design staff. After each person has been assigned a specific task, the lead game designer ensures that the game designs are properly implemented and that development is on schedule and within budget.

A Typical Workday

Working as a video game designer means adapting to new situations on a near daily basis. The tasks designers perform depend

New Tech, New Dreams

"With every game-engine update and game-developer conference comes a wave of new techniques and features. It's impossible to integrate all of them into any individual game—and to make matters worse, video games take years to develop. Even if I start using the latest tech today, it will be three, five, or even more years before it makes it into the hands of players. But that doesn't stop me from dreaming about what kinds of unique gameplay could be developed with each advancement. Each feature becomes a new tool to shape an experience, elicit emotions, and forge new connections with the player."

—Izzy Fiacco, video game designer

Izzy Fiacco, "How Video Game Designers Peek Inside Their Players' Lives," *Slate*, April 29, 2023. https://slate.com.

on the product they are working on, the size of the team, and the various phases of the project. When a new game is proposed, the day begins with a brainstorming session in which designers pitch ideas for various aspects of the game while artists make sketches and storyboards. When a project is in production, there will be long hours of work writing and manipulating computer code to shape the look and feel of the game. This work is interspersed with meetings with other game designers, engineers, and product managers. When projects are nearing completion, designers test games while working to complete the project on time. This can lead to what gaming industry workers call the crunch; periods of eighty-hour workweeks for several months.

Education and Training

Video game designers have an all-consuming passion for playing video games. Their experience as gamers helps them understand how games are structured while providing inspiration for new game ideas. Typically, game designers sketch their ideas on paper or in computer modeling programs. Most game designers develop their drawing abilities in high school and spend time working with graphic design, 3-D modeling, and animation software, such as Autodesk 3ds Max and Maya. Prospective game designers can sign up for online schools like Codecademy or freeCodeCamp, where they can learn popular video game programming languages, including C#, C++, Python, Lua, and Java. Some join game design clubs to discuss and develop ideas for their own games.

Some video game designers are self-taught. But most video game production companies require prospective game designers to hold a bachelor's degree in computer science, game design, software engineering, animation, or a related subject. Degree courses focus on video game design, cover drawing, scripting, 2-D and 3-D modeling, animation, interface design, and storyboard rendering.

Skills and Personality

Video game designers need to meld technical know-how with artistic talent, according to the head of game design at CG Spectrum, Troy Dunniway. He says, "Great art skills will usually make your job as a game designer better—you can use them to either communicate visually, express your ideas, create your own art in-game, or even just know how to modify art that just needs to be tweaked to work properly in a game."[34]

Game designers need to be obsessed with detail. They can spot mistakes even in games designed to confound expert players. Since new game designs have numerous bugs and potential problems, the craft requires a perfectionist who has laser-sharp focus. And games can take several years to finish, which requires game developers to possess a degree of patience rarely required in other fields.

Excellent writing and verbal communication skills are necessary to communicate ideas and keep team members on task. Prospective game designers must also remain current on popular trends in gaming and the gaming industry. Handling multiple duties while designing and coding games is demanding, so designers must maintain a good attitude under pressure.

Workplace Settings

Video game designers work full time in offices and art studios. Some work remotely from home offices. Video game designer Jason W. Bay says his job is not a typical nine-to-five gig: "Since most game employees are salaried workers, there's no punching in and out to track hours. There's a lot of flexibility as to which hours you work and when each employee starts and stops work for the day is up to that employee."[35] But at crunch time, Bay and others are likely to be putting in many extra hours of coding, practice playthroughs, and debugging to ensure a game meets its deadline.

Employers and Pay

Video game designers work for some of the biggest game producers in the world, including Electronic Arts, Activision Blizzard, Microsoft Gaming, and Sony. Smaller companies like Blind Squirrel Games and Team 17, as well as up-and-coming independent studios like Supergiant Games and Heart Machine, also contract with or hire designers. While the industry leaders might be focused on extending successful game franchises, the independents can offer designers more freedom to develop innovative ideas.

The employment website ZipRecruiter says the average annual pay for video game designers was $149,118 in 2025. Game designers who are freelancers or who work for start-ups average $47,000. The highest earners in this sector were bringing in over $160,000 annually, according to ZipRecruiter.

What Is the Future Outlook for Video Game Designers?

In 2025 there were approximately 3.3 billion people playing video games worldwide. There were around 190 million players in the United States—more than 60 percent of the population. This means that the outlook for video game designers is very good. Accordingly, industry sources predict that employment for video game designers will grow by 12 percent through 2030. As long as technology continues to evolve and players demand exciting new games, skilled video game designers will be in demand.

Find Out More

Arts2Work

https://arts2work.media

Arts2Work is an apprenticeship program for those who wish to train as digital media artists without attending college. The organization matches employers to applicants who learn while they earn as entry-level multimedia producers and digital video editors.

CG Spectrum

www.cgspectrum.com

This online video game school features courses in 2-D and 3-D animation, modeling, digital illustration and painting, programming, game design, and related subjects. Visitors to the website can find information about mentors, scholarships, and careers in the gaming industry.

International Game Developers Association (IGDA)

https://igda.org

The IGDA is a nonprofit organization that serves individuals who create video games. Membership is open to both professionals and students who hope to become game developers. The association publishes a newsletter and provides podcasts, career counseling, and a jobs board.

Source Notes

Introduction: Inspiration Occupations

1. Tim Berners-Lee, "Lessons from the Past and Present for the Future of the Web," Knight Foundation, October 29, 2021. https://knightfoundation.org.
2. Quoted in Science+Media Museum, "A Short History of the Internet," December 3, 2020. www.scienceandmediamuseum.org.uk.
3. Liz Marie, "The Good and the Bad of Pursuing a Creative Career," Liz Marie Strategy, 2025. https://lizmariestrategy.com.
4. Liz Marie, "The Good and the Bad of Pursuing a Creative Career."
5. Quoted in Jack Kelly, "Instead of Chasing Happiness at Work, Pursue Purpose and Meaning," *Forbes*, April 4, 2024. www.forbes.com.

Craft Artist

6. Quoted in Pyne & Smith, "A Day in the Life of Alex, a Fiber Artist," 2025. https://pyneandsmith.com.
7. Josie Lewis, "If I Had to Start from Zero with My Art Business," Josie Lewis personal website, 2024. www.josielewis.com.
8. Josie Lewis, "My Story," Josie Lewis personal website, 2024. www.josielewis.com.
9. Serena Archetti, "An Artist Guide to Managing Time," Serena Archetti personal website, April 30, 2024. www.serenaarchetti.com.

Curator

10. Quoted in Job Shadow, "Interview with a Museum Curator," 2025. https://jobshadow.com.
11. Quoted in National Arts Program, "The Art of Curation: Museum Curators Talk About What They Do," 2023. https://nationalartsprogram.org.

12. Quoted in Kelsey Alpaio, "Career Crush: What Does It Take to Be a Museum Curator?," *Harvard Business Review*, December 7, 2021. https://hbr.org.
13. Quoted in Alpaio, "Career Crush."
14. Quoted in Job Shadow, "Interview with a Museum Curator."
15. Quoted in Ashley Mackin Solomon, "La Jolla Car Enthusiast Takes the Wheel as Curator of San Diego Automotive Museum," *San Diego (CA) Union-Tribune*, June 25, 2025. www.sandiegouniontribune.com.

Music Director

16. Joshua Barone, "Gustavo Dudamel: An Introduction in 10 Recordings," *New York Times*, February 7, 2023. www.nytimes.com.
17. Kyle Mattingly, "What Is a Typical Day Like as a Music Composer/Arranger?," CareerVillage.org, May 31, 2022. www.careervillage.org.
18. Quoted in John Knight, "An Interview with Gustavo Dudamel," The Instrumentalist, 2024. https://theinstrumentalist.com.
19. Quoted in Amy Mertz, "A Career in Instrumental Conducting: 7 Key Issues," Majoring in Music, 2024. https://majoringinmusic.com.
20. Quoted in Mertz, "A Career in Instrumental Conducting."

Interior Designer

21. Quoted in Julia Mitchem, "What Do Interior Designers Do?," *Architectural Digest*, 2025. www.architecturaldigest.com.
22. Quoted in Haley Chouinard, "Inside AISD's Fight to Expand Designers' Practice Rights," Business of Home, July 27, 2022. https://businessofhome.com.
23. Quoted in Canvas Rebel, "Meet Tiffany Clark Interior Designer," August 19, 2024. https://canvasrebel.com.
24. Luis Carmona, "Explore the Benefits of Virtual Reality," Beyond Interior Design, 2025. https://beyondidonline.com.
25. Sabina Brandonisio, "Why Interior Designers Benefit from Having a Blog," Sabrina Interiors, 2021. www.sabinainteriors.com.

26. Carmen Brown, "What Is the Day in the Life of an Interior Designer, and How Long Do Projects Usually Take Before You Are Able to See the Finished Product in Person?," Career Village.org, June 26, 2023. www.careervillage.org.

Landscape Designer

27. Rochelle Greayer, "Why I Landscape—a Happy Career Story," Pith+Vigor, October 23, 2023. https://pithandvigor.com.
28. Quoted in Princeton Hydro, "A Day in the Life of Angelica Diaz, Landscape Designer at Princeton Hydro," June 26, 2024. https://princetonhydro.com.
29. Quoted in Donnay Torr, "A Day in the Life of . . . a Landscape Designer," Skills Road, 2025. https://skillsroad.com.
30. Roslyn, "Landscape Architecture and Mathematics," Mathnasium, April 2, 2023. www.mathnasium.com.
31. Scott McLeod, "What Do Landscape Designers Do: Top 7 Crucial Duties in 2024," McLeod Landscaping, June 13, 2024. https://mcleodlandscaping.com.

Video Game Designer

32. Quoted in Mick Lucifer, "In Konversation: Mortal Kombat Online vs John Tobias—Part 1," Mortal Kombat Online, September 16, 2012. www.mortalkombatonline.com.
33. Alexander Brazie, "What Does a Level Designer Do? And How to Become One?," Game Design Skills, 2025. https://gamedesignskills.com.
34. Troy Dunniway, "What Skills Do You Need as a Video Game Designer?," CG Spectrum, 2024. www.cgspectrum.com.
35. Jason W. Bay, "What Is a Typical Day in the Life of a Video Game Developer?," Game Industry Career Guide, 2025. www.gameindustrycareerguide.com.

Interview with a Music Director

Diane Wittry has been the music director and conductor of the Allentown Symphony Orchestra in Pennsylvania since 1995. She has also directed and conducted the Greater Miami Youth Symphony, the Symphony of Southeast Texas, the Norwalk Symphony Orchestra in Connecticut, and the Garden State Philharmonic in New Jersey. The author interviewed Wittry by email.

Q: Why did you decide to become a music director?

A: I fell in love with Conducting when I was a Junior in College. I was a violinist, and I had to take a conducting course to graduate. I felt that conducting an orchestra combined all the things I loved about music making together into one job. The conducting part of the job is very active with the orchestra musicians and the music, while the Music Director part of the job is more administrative with the orchestra board and office staff.

Q: Can you describe your typical workday (or night)?

A: As a Conductor, I do not have a 9:00 to 5:00 position. I spend a lot of time studying scores, and a lot of time in meetings with different committees (Artistic, Education, Board, Executive, and others as needed). If it is concert week, my schedule is full from Thursday through Sunday. On Thursday morning I'll promote the concert with a live radio interview. I'll have lunch with the guest artist and meet with the assistant conductor in the early afternoon. Rehearsals last from 3 until 9:30 pm with a 90-minute break for dinner. Fridays are more-or-less a repeat of Thursdays but with a shorter rehearsal scheduled for the evening. On Saturday we have a dress rehearsal for most of the afternoon before a public performance from 7:00 to 9:30 pm. On Sunday we put on a matinee concert from 2:00 to 4:30 pm.

Q: What do you like most about your job?
A: I really enjoy bringing music to people in new and different ways. I like the way that music can communicate to all different types of people and can change their mood and their life. I also really enjoy working with the musicians and the energy and excitement they bring to all the performances.

Q: What do you like least about your job?
A: All the paperwork and meetings that need to happen so that everything can run smoothly.

Q: What personal qualities do you find most valuable for this type of work?
A: The ability to be flexible and leadership qualities to inspire and bring people together. It is important to have the training and musicianship to present creative musical ideas coherently to musicians and the public. Time management and good organizational skills are a must; we plan 2 years in advance and there are a tremendous number of details involved with any concert.

Q: What advice do you have for students who might be interested in a career as a music director?
A: Get a really good, solid musical foundation on both your main instrument and as a conductor. Learn as much music as you can. Enroll in master class courses. Keep studying and growing as a musician your entire life.

Meet and stay in touch with other people who share the same goals so that you can learn from them and they can help you connect in the industry. Network.

Follow through and be organized and professional with everything you do. Be a person that people can count on.

Always have a great, positive attitude and encourage the best in everyone around you.

Q: What type of projects are you currently working on?

A: I am leaving to teach a conducting master class in the Czech Republic and after that will teach one on Whidbey Island, off the coast of Seattle, WA. I am currently busy preparing and learning the music for the 2025–26 season of the Allentown Symphony and selecting all the music for the 2026–27 season of the Allentown Symphony

I am the author of *Beyond the Baton—What Every Conductor Needs to Know*. I am working on a 2nd edition of this book. I am also working on a new Conducting 101 textbook utilizing ideas and concepts from my conducting technique book *Baton Basics—Communicating Music Through Gestures*.

I also compose music and hope to find some time to write some more pieces. I believe that composing has made me a much better conductor, so I encourage future conductors to also experiment with composing pieces.

Other Jobs If You Like the Creative Arts

Actor
Animator
Announcer
Architect
Art historian
Art therapist
Cartoonist
Choreographer
Comic book artist
Dancer
Fashion designer
Film composer
Film director
Fine artist
Floral designer
Graphic designer
Industrial designer
Instrument builder
Jewelry designer
Model
Musician
Music teacher
Music therapist
Nail artist
Photographer
Package designer
Screen printer
Stylist
Tattoo artist
Textile designer
Theatrical designer
Web developer
Writer

Editor's note: The online *Occupational Outlook Handbook* of the US Department of Labor's Bureau of Labor Statistics is an excellent source of information on jobs in hundreds of career fields, including many of those listed here. The *Occupational Outlook Handbook* may be accessed online at www.bls.gov/ooh.

Index

Picture Credits

Cover: NewAfrica/Shutterstock

10: Monkey Business Images/Shutterstock
19: SeventyFour/Shutterstock
27: Daniel DeSlover/ZUMAPRESS/Newscom
34: Pressmaster/Shutterstock
43: Seventyfour/Shutterstock

About the Author

Stuart A. Kallen is the author of more than four hundred nonfiction books for children and young adults. He has written on topics ranging from the theory of relativity to making a career in the music industry. In 2018 Kallen won a Green Earth Book Award from the Nature Generation environmental organization. He has also written award-winning children's videos and TV scripts. In his spare time, he is a singer, songwriter, and guitarist in San Diego.